A Love for Words: A Collection of Haikus Inspired by My Daughter

Marisol Ramos

BookLeaf Publishing

A Love for Words: A Collection of Haikus Inspired by My Daughter © 2023 Marisol Ramos

Presentation by *BookLeaf Publishing*

Web: www.bookleafpub.com

E-mail: info@bookleafpub.com

ISBN: 9789357440868

First edition 2023

*to flo - you are all of the good parts of me
and the best poem i've ever written*

PREFACE

for christmas my mother gifted me a set of haikubes.

haikubes consist of 63 word cubes - two of which provide the theme for the haiku.

my daughter seemed to love them even more than I did. she's stack them high, line them up along the living room floor, or listen as I read them aloud to her.

and so I thought, why not have her create the poems with me?

I gave her the two themed dice to throw and crafted the haikus based on the luck of her roll. together, we wrote this collection.

a regret about - my family

my brother of love
killed with our dead promises
time to return please

a desire for - my romantic life

sleeping lips on his
moonlight dreaming consume me
glorious places

a reflection on - my childhood

inside my flesh room
the war feeling too heavy
i left this before

a dream about - my future

consume all of me
our fantasy a feeling
for a gentle home

a tirade about - our world

5

its a baby girl!
the simple room slips under
a life so heavy

a vision for - my work life

a lofty fortune
we marvel before my home
who calls but my life?

a regret about - my romantic
life

a finger in me
his ritual ravenous
radical for god

a desire for - our world

8

our ugly journey
it's finally behind us
sweet radical love

a reflection on - my work life

an alternate life
his eyes to my pregnant bump
dripping with that charm

a dream about - our world

my body in waste
empty shelter for trouble
eyes swimming heavy

a tirade about - my romantic
life

you watching me sleep
dripping of desperate waste
never a hero

a vision for - my childhood

she slips between life
i return a happy girl
feeling her fortune

a regret about - my romantic
life

he looks so precious
my partner who spat in me
livid with his love

a desire for - my family

14

a gentle sweet man
he promises my baby
his heart as her home

a reflection on - my romantic
life

he touches my flesh
my melodic partner eats me
wet with promises

a dream about - my future

dancing through the room
your hand finally inside
baby, it's my turn

a tirade about - my work life

revolting villain
we obey a wicked god
desperate for riches

a vision for - my family

i marvel with you
melodic lips on my flesh
fire in our eyes

9 789357 440868